ALL IN FOR HIM

TWENTY-ONE DEVOTIONS FOR COLLEGE ATHLETES: STRENGTHEN YOUR SPIRIT AND BECOME A COMPLETE COMPETITOR

Gwen Thielges

CROSSLINK
PUBLISHING

All In For Him: Twenty-One Devotions for College Athletes:
Strengthen Your Spirit and Become a Complete Competitor

℘
℄ CrossLink Publishing
www.crosslinkpublishing.com

ISBN 978-1-63357-090-0

Library of Congress Control Number: 2016955090

Basketball and sports in general, are great reminders that we can't go through life and/or sports alone. Having great faith assures us that we are not alone and makes our paths brighter along our journeys. Gwen uses real life situations and circumstances to show us how we can use our faith to help us through both the good times as well as bad times, while not compromising our character and integrity along the way.

David J. Richman, Head Men's Basketball Coach,
North Dakota State University

As a Christian coach, I have tried to combine my faith with my sport. All believers know the effect of a strong faith in getting through the ups and downs of life or sport. Gwen Thielges takes many of the special topics an athlete faces and helps them through it. The pressure on athletes these days is great. This devotion will be a calming force in the life of any athlete.

John Stiegelmeier, Head Football Coach,
South Dakota State University

Gwen has written a devotional that should be in the gym bag of every college athlete. As a former sportswriter and college cheerleader, I know the struggles that college athletes face--the struggle of balancing a busy schedule, the pressure of being a good role model, and the drive to be your best even when your best doesn't seem to be good enough, etc. College athletes face many challenges but are also given many opportunities. Having the right mindset is crucial for a successful college experience, and having this book, "All In For Him" will help this gifted group keep their heads on straight and their hearts toward God. It's a must-have!

Michelle Medlock Adams, award-winning & best-selling author of more than 70 books including "Love & Care For the One and Only You: 52 Inspirations"

I have been a coach for over 40 years with 35+ years spent as a head coach at the collegiate level. I have coached hundreds of young men and I was blessed to coach my three sons during a 14 consecutive year span. <u>ALL IN FOR HIM</u> is a tremendous devotional for any collegiate student-athlete and I recommend it without hesitation to all of my former and current 'boys' as well as the young ladies playing collegiate sports. Gwen has addressed important and vital topics in a superior and practical way for every young man and woman. The 'real life' examples and subsequent lessons to be gleaned are scripture based and true to God's word and plan. As a collegiate coach and father, THANK YOU and God bless you for this outstanding, must read devotional.

Scott Berry, Head Baseball Coach,
Mayville State University

"All In For Him" is not just a daily devotional. It is a daily resource for bringing God's Word into the specific experiences an athlete, team, or coach goes through during the season. I especially feel that a college athlete will grow in their relationship with Christ as they read this!

Nathan Stover, Assistant Men's Basketball Coach,
Wayne State College

I have known and worked with countless new young college student-athletes over the span of my coaching career. Gwen's devotional could certainly help students successfully intertwine their faith with their collegiate athletic careers. Interacting daily with God's word and with Him—with the help of this devotional, can help students develop a habit that will serve them well as they continue to grow and mature.

Scott Nagy, Head Men's Basketball Coach,
Wright State University

This devotional is dedicated to my husband, Darren, and to our four children: Tyler, Brady, Drew, and Mallory.

I began writing it in the spring of 2016, a few months before the 2016–2017 school year during which all three of our sons will be participating in college sports, our daughter will be participating in high school basketball, and Darren will be entering his twenty-fifth year of coaching, the last twelve as the head coach of the high school basketball team in our hometown of LaMoure, ND.

This is the year that I will be a mom of three college athletes, which I think of as somewhat of a unique situation. It gave me the inspiration to sit down and write this devotional geared toward college athletes and the issues they face.

My prayer is that if you choose to read this devotional, you will desire a closer relationship with Jesus Christ, you will realize your talent can and should be used to display His glory, and that you will realize what a wonderful opportunity it is to be on an athletic team.

My hope is that you would be grateful for all the experiences you will be a part of during your years as a college athlete. Your thankful spirit will have the potential to impact teammates, coaches, and fans positively for many years into the future.

Spend some quiet time each day the next three weeks with God as you read the twenty-one brief devotions, prayers, and corresponding Bible verses. Let these moments with God remind you of the integral connection between your faith in God and the athletic talent He has blessed you with. Let these moments with God give you a grateful attitude as you take on the potentially life-changing experience of participating in college athletics.

Make a choice to be a student-athlete that is All in for Him!

For from him and through him and for him are all things. To him be the glory forever! Amen. (Romans 11:36)

Table of Contents

PRAYER FOR THE
BEGINNING OF THE SEASON

Dear Lord, I thank you that I am about to begin a season of college athletics. I have some expectations in my mind, but in all honesty… I do not know how everything will pan out. I am about to begin a new chapter of unknowns. However, may I always remember that there are some things that I will always know: You are with me, You love me, and You have great plans for me. You are constant. You are an everlasting, eternal God in a world of instantaneous decisions and immediate gratification.

Lord, I want to do what I can do and leave the rest up to You! Help me in my desire to do that. I can control how hard I work, what kind of an attitude I have, and how coachable I am. After that, I have to find a way to allow the rest of the pieces to fall into place, and allow Romans 8:28 to come to fruition." "We know that all things work together for good for those who love God, who are called according to his purpose."

I do not want to take for granted that I have been given the option to compete in a sport I love at a high level of competition. I do not want to take for granted that I get to be part of a team that is purposefully laboring together toward a shared goal. Many people would love to experience this; help me remember that when there are obstacles and difficulties. Help me to see that obstacles and difficulties are opportunities to see how You will guide me through them.

My prayer is that I will glorify You during this sports season, Lord. I pray that I will reflect Your nature no matter what I am faced with. Whether I am in the midst of a sports season of success or disappointment or a combination of the two, may I remember that my relationship with You is paramount. Nothing else is as important or fulfilling.

Help me to continue to be thankful for this precious life experience. May others see a grateful spirit in me, in my actions, and in my words.

Lord, I pray for this season to be one that will be remembered as a time of spiritual breakthrough in my life. My genuine desire is to become closer to You, Lord.

In Your holy name I pray, Amen.

For he will command his angels concerning you to guard you in all your ways. (Psalm 91:11)

There is a time for everything, and a season for every activity under the heavens. (Ecclesiastes 3:1)

You make known to me the path of life; you will fill me with joy in your presence, with eternal pleasures at your right hand. (Psalm 16:11)

REDSHIRTS AND ROLE PLAYERS

M any college athletes go through a redshirt year at college. It is a year of putting forth much effort gaining speed and strength to become more prepared to compete at the college level.

It is a difficult year for various reasons, one of them being that many college players are accustomed to being a starter or even a star player in high school. Suddenly, they are just one of many stars waiting for their time to get an opportunity to shine.

Another reason "redshirting" is difficult is that they are expected to continue a strenuous training program without seemingly seeing the benefits that the other players experience.

Even though they are a part of the team, they are a unique part of the team. It takes an extra amount of perseverance and persistence to keep envisioning the future beyond that year in a positive light. Many players enter college knowing that they may not see the field until their third or fourth year.

I remember overhearing a conversation between two high school athletes, both starters on their successful basketball team. They were talking about how their team would have never had the season they had were it not for the scout squad at practice. They were very complimentary of the talent of their teammates and were grateful for the caliber of competition they provided at practice. They realized the all-out effort of the second string forced the starters to put in harder work, and therefore the entire team benefitted.

If you are a redshirt or a role player, you are going to receive reactions different from what the star players receive. It can be an exercise in humility. It can also be a time to reflect as to why you are playing college sports. If it is for the fame or the feeling of importance, then it may be time to rethink your motivation!

If you keep reminding yourself that you are competing for an Audience of One and that your wholehearted effort as a redshirt, role player, or as a star player—whatever the case may be—makes a positive difference to the entire makeup of the team, you will definitely be practicing and playing with a Christlike mindset.

I can do all this through him who gives me strength. (Philippians 4:13)

So whether you eat or drink or whatever you do, do it all for the glory of God. (1 Corinthians 10:31)

"For I know the plans I have for you," declares the LORD, "plans to prosper you and not to harm you, plans to give you hope and a future." (Jeremiah 29:11)

Dear Lord, every team is composed of players with different skill sets and contributions. Lord, I want to be ready physically and mentally to fill any role that the coaches ask me to. Help me be prepared to be an asset to the team; to assist in functioning at its highest potential no matter what contribution I am expected to make. In Your holy name I pray, Amen.

THINK ON
THESE THINGS

Have you ever spent time with a teammate who seemingly spends most of their time complaining? Maybe the negative comments are about coaches, other teammates, or maybe they are about circumstances. Regardless of the topic, negative thinking that turns into negative conversation can certainly bring down the morale of the team.

Many of us have been influenced by that type of team member before, and if we are not cautious and aware of what is happening, we can become that type of person as well.

Given the option of listening to a stream of negative comments or inspiration, my unscientific guess is that 99 percent of people would choose the positive teammates! We should certainly strive to be the kind of teammate that others want to spend time with, as they know that they will be encouraged and enthused rather than discouraged and disheartened!

What we say is an overflow of what is in our heart. Therefore, what we spend our time concentrating on should definitely be the positives in our lives. Philippians 4:8 sums it up quite well: "Finally, brothers and sisters, whatever is true, whatever is noble, whatever is right, whatever is pure, whatever is lovely, whatever is admirable—if anything is excellent or praiseworthy—think about such things."

The Bible says that we have been given self-discipline (2 Timothy 1:7), that our mind can be renewed (Romans 12:2), and that we can have the mind of Christ (1 Corinthians 2:16). None of these promises should be taken lightly. They are real, and they are ours to accept. When we use excuses such as, "I can't control my thoughts," or "I just can't stop thinking about that," we are actually doubting the power of God to help us in our thought life. God desires to help us in every aspect of our lives!

Be the teammate that brings the mood in the locker room or the playing field back up with positive words that stem from positive thoughts.

Finally, brothers and sisters, whatever is true, whatever is noble, whatever is right, whatever is pure, whatever is lovely, whatever is admirable—if anything is excellent or praiseworthy—think about such things. (Philippians 4:8)

Be kind and compassionate to one another, forgiving each other, just as in Christ God forgave you. (Ephesians 4:32)

Do not conform to the pattern of this world, but be transformed by the renewing of your mind. Then you will be able to test and approve what God's will is—his good, pleasing and perfect will. (Romans 12:2)

Dear Lord, I pray that You will help me think on what is true, noble, right, pure, lovely and admirable. I truly desire to have the "mind of Christ." I know that You can help me and that You want to help me think on what is excellent and praiseworthy. Thank You, Lord, for being concerned about everything in my life, including what I spend my time thinking about. May I realize just how much that matters and how much it affects me and others around me. In Your holy name I pray, Amen.

BODY LANGUAGE

S ince my husband is a coach, I have often heard him talk about the body language of the players on his team and on other teams as well. He notices when shoulders slump and heads hang. These are not the actions of a winning player on a winning team!

We have all seen it before: one team goes on a scoring run, and the other team is seemingly doing all they can do to prevent it from getting out of hand. At first, they stay motivated and attempt to encourage each other with high-fives and pats on the back. However, as the hole gets deeper and a realization that defeat may be on the horizon takes hold, body language changes. Eyes look downward in self-defeat or eyes roll as the blame is placed on teammates.

A point guard who throws his hands up because a post just missed his no-look pass makes the game about him. It is a "Look at ME—my teammates have let me down" type of attitude that tries to elicit pity from the fans. Even a player who does not blame others but instead looks down in shame after she misses a block makes the game about her.

Teammates who continue to nod, high-five, pump fists, and keep their heads up are often crowd favorites. Their enthusiasm is contagious.

As a fan, I can attest to the fact that seeing players who encourage each other can sway my allegiance from one team to the other.

Sharp words said to each other in the heat of competition cannot necessarily be heard from the bleachers, but the unspoken language communicated by physical actions speaks loudly and oh-so-clearly!

Be the player that your teammates can depend on to carry him or herself in a positive and uplifting manner. Be the player that your coaches can rely upon to look them in the eyes with respect even when you might disagree with their game plan or the fact that you are being sternly reminded that you did not do your job on the field.

Be the player that points others to Jesus.

Therefore encourage one another and build each other up, just as in fact you are doing. (1 Thessalonians 5:11)

Do to others as you would have them do to you. (Luke 6:31)

Be completely humble and gentle; be patient, bearing with one another in love. (Ephesians 4:2)

Dear Lord, You have blessed me with the opportunity to play college sports for Your glory. May my body language toward my teammates, coaches, and opponents display that I know Who You truly are. May Your humility and love be seen in my actions toward others. In Your holy name I pray, Amen.

RESPECTING AUTHORITY

I n typical families, young children are taught to respect authority. Parents teach their children to obey them. Children are told to listen to their teachers and to behave in class. As we get older, conventional wisdom tells us we should be listening to our elders and respecting the advice of those who have already been through what we have not yet gone through. Although it can be argued that respect for authority is on the decline in some situations, it is still thought of as the norm.

As a college athlete, how do you rate yourself in the "showing respect for authority" department? Most likely you follow the training rules, you make it to practice on time, and you have high regard for your coaches' knowledge of the game. But...how about when coaches favor less-talented players than you? How about when coaches do not seem to reward your effort? How about when trainers give more "attaboys" and "attagirls" to players who do not work as hard as or put in as much time as you? How about when officials clearly make the wrong call? How about when officials seemingly target you?

Have you ever been in any of those situations and wondered how you can be expected to show respect to authority figures who have done something that caused you to lose some of the respect you had for them in the first place?

One important step is to remind yourself of the enormous responsibility that coaches, trainers, and officials have. Remember that they are dealing with more than just your situation. Coaches and trainers are striving to build a strong program made up of many different skill sets, personalities, and talents. An official's job is trying to call an unbiased game in front of biased crowd members. Stepping back and seeing things from their perspective may prove that they do, in fact, deserve more respect than you previously thought!

However, there will be times when you have to make a choice to be respectful even if you do not feel like it! It is a sign of class and maturity when you put personal opinions aside and respond in a levelheaded, gracious manner toward authority figures whom you disagree with. Pray that God will give you the ability to see the situation in an unbiased way and to show respect at all times.

Be devoted to one another in love. Honor one another above yourselves. (Romans 12:10)

In everything set them an example by doing what is good. In your teaching show integrity, seriousness. (Titus 2:7)

Do nothing out of selfish ambition or vain conceit. Rather, in humility value others above yourselves. (Philippians 2:3)

Dear Lord, help me to respect all those in authority over me. I ask You to give me the desire to conduct myself in a Christlike manner whether I am in complete agreement or total disagreement with my coaches, trainers, officials, and all other authority figures. May I be a Godly example. In Your holy name I pray, Amen.

MAKE IT OR BRING IT...
A NEW LEVEL

Many thanks to my husband, Darren, for writing this guest devotional. He was a college athlete, and he has been a high school coach for many years.

As a college athlete, it is safe to say that you accomplished many things up to this point. You worked hard to be the leader of your high school team. Your hard work earned the respect and admiration of your coaches, teammates, and community. You were probably courted by college coaches and your opposition knew who you were!

Now after all the tough practices, time commitment, workouts, games, and long bus rides… somehow, high school is over and you are in college. It is a time to reflect.

After reflecting, a moment will come when you are forced to look at what will be; the moment when you have moved past the ending point and have reached a new starting point. How will people like me? How will I achieve status? More questions than answers fill your mind and most center around: "How can I fit in?"

Many possible answers will be offered as soon as you set foot on campus. Most solutions will present themselves as: You will make it if you just _____. Any answer in this blank is a response to an already established normal. But what if you want to be better than normal? What if there is the possibility for more than is already there? What if you want the best?

Maybe a better question to answer is: "What can I bring to this campus?"

You see, the very gifts that God placed in you to be seen and noticed in high school are the same gifts you can bring to your college. God did His part. Give of yourself rather than getting for yourself. If your focus is on getting what you deserve, what compromises and shortcuts will you be willing to make and take to put yourself in that position? If you instead give of yourself, you are bringing something that positively influences others around you and enhances the existing culture. The focus isn't on an end—it is on the process.

By bringing it, in contrast to making it, you will:

1. Be proactive rather than reactive.
2. Be encouraging rather than discouraging.
3. Be positive rather than negative.
4. Be adding to rather than taking from.
5. Be a team rather than an individual.

When your ultimate goal is "making it," the temptation to take others down presents itself as an option. When your goal is "bringing it," you elevate yourself and others to be the best. By bringing it, you can be successful every day regardless of the score of the game. Every day there will be new challenges, and the reward is being your best and your team being the best without having to bring someone else down.

Give, and it will be given to you. A good measure, pressed down, shaken together and running over, will be poured into your lap. For with the measure you use, it will be measured to you. (Luke 6:38)

For the LORD God is a sun and shield; the LORD bestows favor and honor; no good thing does he withhold from those whose walk is blameless. LORD Almighty, blessed is the one who trusts in you. (Psalm 84:11–12)

Dear Lord, help me to use the gifts You have given me for Your glory. May I not be focused on "making it" but instead on "bringing it." I know You have a plan for me to contribute to the team in the best way possible in order to bring You honor. In Your holy name I pray, Amen.

PRAYER FOR COACHES

Dear Lord, I lift my coaches to You. I thank You for their desire to work with athletes and to see them improve and better themselves. I thank You for their willingness to invest time and energy in athletic programs and athletes that participate. I thank You for the sacrifices that they make in their personal lives to strive to do the best they can in their professional lives.

I pray my coaches seek wisdom in the numerous decisions they must make on a daily basis. Help them seek You for wisdom in how they work with others, how they run their program, and how to instruct their team members. Lord, help me respect the many responsibilities that my coaches are accountable for throughout the season and the off-season.

I want to be a player that my coaches see as coachable and responsive. Lord, help me to be a team member they can depend upon to be a hard worker, a positive example, and a relentless competitor. I pray that when they think of me, they will be grateful I am part of their team.

I pray I will treat them with respect even if there are times that I do not agree with or understand their decisions. Help me remember they are attempting to make decisions based on the betterment of an entire team, not individuals. I desire to be a player on their team who promotes team unity and does not take part in any potential divisions. Lord, help me speak highly of my coaches to others and open my eyes to all of their positive attributes.

Dear Lord, help my coaches to have a renewed zest and enthusiasm for their job. Their commitments as a coach, mentor, teacher, and sometimes even counselor can be exhausting. Reinvigorate and reenergize my coaches.

Lord, I pray for my coaches to have a personal relationship with You. If they do not have one, may they see their need for a Savior. I pray they will receive a glimpse of Who You are through the way I treat them, my teammates, and others. If they do have a personal relationship with You, I pray the way I act will be a catalyst for them to seek an even closer relationship with You.

Dear Lord, I thank You again for my coaches and pray for this year to be a year of breakthrough for their spiritual life, family life, and in their jobs. Thank You for loving them, and I pray they will feel Your presence and Your love in their lives.

In Your holy name I pray, Amen.

I urge, then, first of all, that petitions, prayers, intercession *and* thanksgiving be made for all people – for kings and all those in authority, that we may live peaceful and quiet lives in all godliness and holiness. This is good, and pleases God our Savior, who wants all people to be saved and to come to a knowledge of the truth. (1 Timothy 2:1-4)

In the same way, you who are younger, submit yourselves to your elders. All of you, clothe yourselves with humility toward one another, because, "God opposes the proud but shows favor to the humble." (1 Peter 5:5)

HUMILITY AND GODLY CONFIDENCE

L et's be honest. Watching professional athletes and other celebrities can sometimes remind us that this world is lacking humility. There is a pervasive "It's all about me" mentality. There are moments when it is valid to think that giving others credit is seemingly a lost art.

An interview monopolized with the words "I" and "me" as opposed to highlighting the contributions of teammates, support of family, and wisdom of coaches is an obvious example of a vain attitude. In contrast, when a quarterback praises his offensive line for preventing sacks, and when a post is grateful to his perimeter teammates for seeing when he is open, we know they are players who possess a humble mindset.

There is, however, a point at which athletes can actually go overboard with the concept of humility. When they refuse to accept compliments and wave off positive feedback, they are taking humility to an unhealthy extreme! An inferiority complex happens when we forget that God has created us as His most brilliant creation. God has given college athletes a talent that is to be used to showcase His glory. It is definitely difficult for His glory to shine through a vessel drowning in low self-esteem issues!

False humility comes into play when athletes take part in the activity known as 'fishing for compliments." I am sure you have seen it before: a teammate talks about how badly they have been playing in order to coax listeners to heap flattery upon them and say that they are being too hard on themselves.

True humility is a Christlike trait, one we are expected to pursue. Back to my original point: humility is Godly confidence that He can work through you when you allow Him to!

Our third son remembers looking up to certain athletes in his formative years and noticing the ones who worked hard without seeking recognition. He admired that quality and observed they gained the respect of officials and fans alike. When he became a varsity athlete, he took that responsibility seriously and endeavored to be an example worthy of following. Compliments he, his father, and I receive about his humble nature are evidence that he has done a commendable job reaching this goal.

As you pursue your college sports career, make a choice to remember Whom your talents come from and Whom the glory goes to!

Take my yoke upon you and learn from me, for I am gentle and humble in heart, and you will find rest for your souls. (Matthew 11:29)

Who is wise and understanding among you? Let them show it by their good life, by deeds done in the humility that comes from wisdom. (James 3:13)

When pride comes, then comes disgrace, but with humility comes wisdom. (Proverbs 11:2)

Dear Lord, I ask for Your help as I try to follow Your wonderful example of humility. Please give me the right words and actions that will demonstrate that I thank You for this opportunity, and that I want the honor and glory to go directly to You. May I receive compliments and critiques graciously. In Your holy name I pray, Amen.

SACRIFICE

S ome college athletes are seemingly driven to spend numerous extra hours on the court, on the field, and in the weight room. Are you that type of player?

When friends are planning a group outing, are you the one who sits out in order to put up some extra shots in the gym or take some extra cuts at the batting cage? Are you the player who watches your diet and puts your sleep schedule above your social schedule, because you have learned through the years that healthy, well-rested athletes have more success?

We have all admired the players who earn the "hardest worker" awards, the ones who go the extra mile and motivate their teammates to do the same. While you can make a decision to be that type of player, there is much more to it than that. A decision must be made to make sacrifices. It is a decision to put others before yourself. It is a decision to put the team above the individual.

When you first see the weightlifting schedule the summer before your first college season of competitive sports, you may wonder when you will possibly enjoy the usual summer activities of going to the lake, swimming, and hanging out with friends. In order to maintain a schedule that includes training, a job, preparing for college, possibly summer school, getting a good night's rest, and other responsibilities, it takes some definite prioritizing and planning.

In the midst of a hectic college schedule, choices of how to use your time efficiently must be made on a daily basis. It is not easy when you are answering to coaches, professors, and possibly a boss, if you hold down a job. However, wise choices can always be made, because we serve a God who says we can go to Him for wisdom in all things. James 1:5 says, "If any of you lacks wisdom, you should ask God, who gives generously to all without finding fault, and it will be given to you." He will help you figure out how to keep a schedule that offers your best self to all of your commitments, your friends, your family, and most importantly, God.

But those who hope in the LORD will renew their strength. They will soar on wings like eagles; they will run and not grow weary, they will walk and not be faint. (Isaiah 40:31)

Commit to the LORD whatever you do, and he will establish your plans. (Proverbs 16:3)

Therefore, I urge you, brothers and sisters, in view of God's mercy, to offer your bodies as a living sacrifice, holy and pleasing to God—this is your true and proper worship. (Romans 12:1)

Dear Lord, You have blessed me with the ability and opportunity to play a college sport. It takes tremendous commitment, time, and effort. I cannot possibly do it on my own. I ask You for Your help, and I thank You for giving me the wisdom to prioritize my time. Thank You, Lord, for Your many blessings. In Your holy name I pray, Amen.

BEING A
ROLE MODEL

R eady or not, asked-for or not, there are going to be eyes watching your behavior on and off the playing field. It is, as they say, "part of the package" when you become a college athlete.

I do not know if you are someone who thrives on potentially being looked up to or instead, tries to completely steer clear of that attention. Some athletes love the spotlight. Others would be much happier if their conduct was not being critiqued, criticized, or copied, whatever the case may be.

I have always wanted our children to know that what it boils down to is that they are living their lives for an Audience of One. I pray they desire to do their best to please God in all they do and say. If they strive to do that, there is no guarantee they won't be criticized. However, there is a guarantee that their behavior is worth copying!

There may be peers or younger children who look to you as a role model. While that may put pressure on you, it is of the positive kind! It is a compliment, and if you are striving to live a faith-filled Christian life, then it can be something you welcome! As our daughter has said, knowing you have made an impact on someone in the past keeps you aware of your actions for the future in a positive way. She is in high school and in view of peers and younger kids alike. She is active in basketball, choir, band, Fellowship of Christian Athletes, and student council among other activities. It gives her a great feeling that there is a strong possibility of her being a good influence on others.

As you think about how you are carrying yourself on or off the field, remember that God's opinion is the one that genuinely matters, and it should be your true motivator. If you are striving to please Him in the way you live your life, then you are setting an awesome example for anyone who might follow your lead.

Don't let anyone look down on you because you are young, but set an example for the believers in speech, in conduct, in love, in faith and in purity. (1 Timothy 4:12)

In the same way, let your light shine before others, that they may see your good deeds and glorify your Father in heaven. (Matthew 5:16)

Follow my example, as I follow the example of Christ. (1 Corinthians 11:1)

Dear Lord, may my behavior be worthy of being modeled by those who look up to and admire me. I pray I will always look to You for wisdom and as an example of how I can live a life filled with Your love, mercy, and grace. In Your holy name I pray. Amen

THE
FINAL PLAY

When the game is on the line, are you the player who wants the ball in your hands? Would you rather be in the mix but not responsible for the scoring effort? Or would you rather not be on the court or the field, therefore not having to answer if it turns out to be a failed attempt to seize the victory?

In my husband's years of basketball coaching experience, there have been times when he has had to draw up last-minute plans to put his team in the best position to put points on the scoreboard and pull off the win. He has always known which players had the composure and talent required to handle the pressure of that eleventh-hour effort.

Our second son is the type of player who thrives on opportunities to compete at a high level. When he was a scoring guard on the basketball team and a running back on the football team in high school, he was known for having that competitive edge. He welcomed the opportunity to be the "go-to guy." On his college football team, he is a defensive back, so his desire has shifted to preventing the other team from scoring. He has said that when his best is needed, he wants to be at his best so that he can do his best! Therefore, he has labored on and off the field to improve and prove his abilities. When the opportunity arises for him to be on the field for the last-ditch effort of the opposing team, he will put forth his greatest effort to prevent, deflect, or intercept the winning touchdown. His work ethic will provide him with confidence in his skills, and as he has expressed, the trust his teammates have in him will give him courage.

If you are the type of player who flourishes when your teammates are relying on you, you will hope that your coaches call upon you to be a playmaker. Even with the adrenaline rush and the understandable nerves that last-second game-winning attempts cause, you want your number called! Remember that God can give you poise and peace to handle those final play situations in a way that points others to Him!

Peace I leave with you; my peace I give you. I do not give to you as the world gives. Do not let your hearts be troubled and do not be afraid. (John 14:27)

When I am afraid, I put my trust in you. (Psalm 56:3)

"Whoever can be trusted with very little can also be trusted with much, and whoever is dishonest with very little will also be dishonest with much. (Luke 16:10)

Dear Lord, when the coach looks to me to be a playmaker in the final seconds, I pray for a calm to come over me that only You can offer. Whether the last-ditch effort is successful or not, may I put my best foot forward and show class in both victory and defeat. The attitude I have toward playing in a high-pressure situation has an impact on my teammates, coaches, and fans. May I never take it lightly. May others see a glimpse of You in me. In Your holy name I pray, Amen.

Internet/Social Media
Part 1

What is the first thing you do when you wake up in the morning? Check your Twitter? Read your emails? Inspect your missed texts? Examine your Facebook notifications? It seems numerous people wake up to quickly see what they missed while they were sleeping after they have done a final run-through of social media on their phones right before they turned in for the night.

I am not anti-social media or internet. It has its place, its positives, and its perks. Unfortunately, it also has its pitfalls, its perils, and its problems.

One of those problems is the faux bravery it provides. Some college athletes have been targeted by opinionated Twitter users and have found themselves involved in unnecessary drama with someone who is tucked safely behind their screens. People can openly share their opinions regarding the skill level, personality, or even the wardrobe, of others. We must guard against being impacted by words of someone who does not know us or the whole story.

The internet can also dominate our time. Have you experienced a time when you intended to do "a quick check of Twitter" and it turned into hours of mindless internet surfing? There is nothing wrong with surfing the internet or posting updates, but when it is what our day is built around, it becomes a problem. When we are endlessly *favoriting*, commenting, snap chatting, googling, and tweeting instead of carrying on conversations face-to-face or engaging in real-life activities, we have made a choice to allow it to control us. If God looked at an hour-by-hour schedule of what you did yesterday, where would He think your priorities are?

There are two steps we can take to avoid the potential drawbacks of the internet.

First, be diligent in identifying who you are in God's eyes. God sees you as the "apple of His eye." What people say to you or about you on a screen does not change what your Heavenly Father says about you. He created you on purpose, for a purpose, and granted you gifts that will help you live out His plan for your life.

Also, start your day by saturating yourself in God's Word instead of technology. Imagine the change in our perspective if we would begin our day with reminders of His unfailing love instead of reminders from our online calendar.

As you go through your day looking for ways to glorify Him, include your use of the internet. Put Him first!

Teach us to number our days that we may gain a heart of wisdom. (Psalm 90:12)

Keep me as the apple of your eye; hide me in the shadow of your wings. (Psalm 17:8)

Be very careful, then, how you live—not as unwise but as wise. (Ephesians 5:15)

Dear Lord, help me to use my time wisely; to take part in activities that will help me to be a better person, student, and athlete. And help me to only rely on what You say about me, Lord. I ask for Your wisdom. In Your holy name I pray, Amen.

INTERNET/SOCIAL MEDIA PART 2

Yesterday, I spoke of two negatives about the internet. Today I will address one more.

The ease in which inappropriate images are accessed, whether you are seeking them out or not, is a definite problem that the internet presents to us. Obviously numerous people go to pornographic sites, but unwanted images can flash across the screen even when you are engaged in an innocent internet activity.

Seeking images that cause us to see other people as objects or as a means to bring gratification is a dangerous pitfall to fall into. When we look at others, our goal should be to see them as Jesus does. Pornographic or suggestive images twist the way in which we think about others, see others, and ultimately how we treat others. In a world where people are told that pornography is okay, now is the time to see the stress and sorrow that it causes, and it is time to stand up for what Jesus wants for us.

Is pornography something that can be dabbled in? No, I am afraid not. We are visual creatures, and those images remain in our minds and affect our thoughts. If we have run across suggestive sites, whether innocently or not, images are extremely difficult to remove from our minds, but we can ask God to replace those ideas and scenes with thoughts that honor Him.

Think about the direction your mind goes when you are faced with an inappropriate image. Do your thoughts become more worshipful and wise, or do they begin to take you down a path in which God is not glorified? Do you find yourself setting your mind on things above, as we are told to in Colossians 3:2?

As Christians, we are to be striving to live as He has instructed us. It is important to realize His good and perfect plan for our lives. Remember that God expects us to reserve sex for a married relationship; one which has started with vows to God and each other.... He is not interested in withholding something from us in our dating years, rather He is hoping to bless us with something amazing in our marriage. These images dishonor what God has given to us as a gift.

The internet can have many uses. Make the choice to use it in a way that brings you closer to HIM!

Set your minds on things above, not on earthly things. (Colossians 3:2)

That is why a man leaves his father and mother and is united to his wife, and they become one flesh. (Genesis 2:24)

Do not conform to the pattern of this world, but be transformed by the renewing of your mind. Then you will be able to test and approve what God's will is—his good, pleasing and perfect will. (Romans 12:2)

Dear Lord, we are faced with choices every day of our lives. We do not desire to be passive ... we want to be active in making the decisions that will glorify You. Help us flee from any image that taints our impression of others. May we see others with Your eyes, Lord. In Your holy name I pray, Amen.

WHEN YOU ARE THE UNDERDOG

Whether it is statistically speaking, historically speaking, or athletically speaking, there may be an upcoming game when one team is highly favored to beat their opponents. Many times, analysts and fans have the game already played out and decided on paper before the visiting team has even arrived. However, as the cliché goes, "That's why they play the game," and many "once-in-a-lifetime games have been won by the underdog team because they refused to lose!

Being a member of the "David team" can be a tough situation when a David vs. Goliath game is on the upcoming schedule. When your team is not expected to win, maintaining a positive attitude is especially difficult. Practicing and preparing in the face of seemingly insurmountable odds is a test in being courageous, calm, and composed. A conscious decision must be made by each player to believe in their own abilities and the abilities of their teammates if they are going to make a solid attempt at claiming victory.

When you believe that you and your teammates are capable of overcoming the odds together and the game ends in your favor, it is a valuable, memorable experience. As the years go by, it is almost guaranteed that particular unforgettable game will be brought up when trying to motivate someone who is lacking in confidence.

When each team member outworks and outhustles the opposing team, even losing those types of games can be a cherished memory. They are builders of team confidence and team unity. Years later, memories will continue: "Remember when we almost pulled it off?" "Can you believe we almost had them?"

Asking God to help you always put forth your best effort and to help you to possess an attitude of perseverance in the face of adversity is important! When you present a Godly attitude in wins and in losses, you display a glimpse of His nature! That can make a lasting impact on your teammates, coaches, and fans. What a blessing to be able to use your talents and passion for athletics to exhibit the qualities of God to others. And…what a responsibility. Be ready to reflect God's character no matter what challenge awaits you and your team.

Trust in the Lord with all your heart, and lean not on your own understanding; in all your ways submit to him, and He will make your paths straight. (Proverbs 3:5–6)

Stand firm, and you will win life. (Luke 21:19)

Dear Lord, I pray that others will see You in the way I persevere, encourage others, and strive to play to the best of my ability no matter what the scoreboard says. Help me to reflect You in wins, losses, and preparation for all types of games. I pray that others will see You through my attitude. In Your holy name I pray, Amen.

Prayer Before the Big Game

D ear Lord, I come to you today and ask you to be with me. I pray that I will feel Your presence with me as the hours tick closer to the tipoff of this game.

First, I want to thank You for giving me this opportunity to compete. I am grateful to You for giving me good health, terrific teammates, exceptional coaches, and supportive family and friends. I am thankful for the family members and high school coaches and others who made this college athletic experience a possibility in my life. May I forever be impacted for the better by these college years.

Lord, our team and our coaches have purposefully prepared for this contest today. We have discussed and honed our strategy, we have watched film, and we have put in many hours of practicing different game scenarios. I pray the game preparation comes together in an unforgettable way today as we play to the best of our abilities.

I pray that You will help the coaches make wise game-time decisions, and that the players will buy into the game plan that has been developed with us in mind. I pray for clarity for me and for my teammates as we make split-second decisions during the course of the game. Help us think about the team as a whole and about what our shared goals are. Lord, I ask You to give us a confidence in each other as we put forth our best effort today.

Lord, I pray that You will keep us free from injury and sickness. I pray for the health and the protection of all teams participating today. Please, keep teams and fans safe as they travel today.

You have gifted me with determination and a desire to compete. Your Word says that whatever we do we should do it all for Your glory. Lord, I pray that my abilities and achievements will never be about me, but instead about showing who You are. I ask that any success my team enjoys displays Your glory and draws people's eyes to Your abilities and Your power.

Lord, You have granted me an amazing opportunity today, and may I never take any game for granted. May the manner in which I passionately compete, cheer on my teammates, and treat everyone involved in this game in a respectful way inspire others to know You better.

In Your holy name I pray, Amen.

The Lord makes firm the steps of the one who delights in him; though he may stumble, he will not fall, for the Lord upholds him with his hand. (Psalm 37:23-24)

So do not fear, for I am with you; do not be dismayed, for I am your God. I will strengthen you and help you; I will uphold you with my righteous right hand. (Isaiah 41:10)

PRAYER
FOR TEAMMATES

D ear Lord, I lift my teammates to You. I pray that they will be assured of Your constant, faithful presence. I pray that You will make Yourself so very real to them, and that You will take away any doubts they may have about Who You are.

Thank You for the circumstances that have made it possible for me to spend time with and get to know my teammates. What an awesome opportunity it is to be in a new situation with new people; to have friendships with and to gain admiration for these new teammates. Although there may be times when conflicts arise because of the amount of time we spend together, I pray that we will always treat each other with respect. Lord, help us settle disagreements in a mature manner that enhances our relationship. Tensions may appear at times, as is typical in groups of people who are working together toward a common goal. Lord, please be there for us and guide us on the path of peace and understanding.

One of my most sincere prayers is that You will draw closer to my teammates, and that You will give them a desire to draw closer to You. I pray they will realize how important it is to have a personal relationship with You and to place You number one in their lives.

I pray they will have a fervent, sincere desire to deepen their faith through prayer, worship, and reading Your Holy Word. Lord, give them a desire for a mature spiritual life, and may I be an example of someone that is pursuing a deeper spiritual life as well.

When their souls need refreshment, grant it to them, Lord. I ask You to help me be a source of encouragement and positivity for them in times of need. Help me be one of the reasons that they continue going forward when they may feel like giving up.

Lord, I pray for my teammates to continue improving; to get stronger, to get faster, to be free from injury, and to continue working on their individual skills. I pray they will be focused on being a unifying presence for our team, and that they will make team-oriented choices. Lord, help me and all of my teammates to be counted upon to make selfless decisions.

Dear Lord, I pray that you will help me develop genuine friendships with the athletes I am blessed to compete with. Thank You for each and every teammate I have, and may I always be someone that points them to You and Your love.

In Your holy name I pray, Amen.

Two are better than one, because they have a good return for their labor: If either of them falls down, one can help the other up. But pity anyone who falls and has no one to help them up. Also, if two lie down together, they will keep warm. But how can one keep warm *alone*? Though one may be overpowered, two can defend themselves. A cord of three *strands* is not quickly broken. (Ecclesiastes 4:9-12)

And we urge you, brothers and sisters, warn those who are idle and disruptive, encourage the disheartened, help the weak, be patient with everyone. (1 Thessalonians 5:14)

LEADING
AND FOLLOWING

E very successful team is full of players who not only understand their roles, but enthusiastically embrace them as well.

Sometimes the role a person is called upon to fulfill is that of leader. Leaders come in all shapes and sizes, and they definitely come in many different styles. Coaches see value in the vocal, get-in-the-faces-of-their-teammates types of leaders, but they appreciate the nonvocal, lead-by-example types also. Those types of leaders have numerous subcategories underneath them as well.

Our oldest son has been referred to as a 'born leader' by former coaches. He is the type of player who thrives on rising up to challenges in his path. He falls into the more vocal category of leadership, and he has emphasized that a large part of successful leadership is "doing the right thing especially when it is hard." He also has coaching experience, and he works hard to develop leaders in his program, teaching them by words and example what it means to inspire trust in their teammates.

Working out when you are mentally or physically tired, keeping a positive attitude when the game is not going the way you had hoped, and practicing with the same passion and energy as you play in a game with are characteristics of leaders who gain the esteem of teammates and coaches.

In order to be known as a leader, you must have people willing to follow! Teammates must believe those in leadership positions will strive to guide and motivate them in ways that bring improvement and unity to the team.

Maybe you are being called upon to be a leader. Maybe you are being called upon to be a loyal follower. Regardless of your role, make a decision today to accept and carry out your role in a manner that reflects Christ.

So in everything, do to others what you would have them do to you, for this sums up the Law and the Prophets. (Matthew 7:12)

And David shepherded them with integrity of heart; with skillful hands he led them. (Psalm 78:72)

Pride brings a person low, but the lowly in spirit gain honor. (Proverbs 29:23)

Dear Lord, You have blessed all of us with various skills that are to be used for Your glory. Whether my abilities manifest themselves in being more of a leader or a follower, I pray You will help me to refine and sharpen my skills toward the betterment of this team. Lord, help me to act in a way that abides with the game plan of our coaches. Help me to be an example of how to lead or how to follow with respect and dignity! Lord, my desire is to be a team member who enhances the makeup of this team by wholly embracing my part. In Your holy name I pray, Amen.

FOURTH
QUARTER

I t is the fourth quarter, the ninth inning, or the last period. Quick! What is your battle cry?

For some it is, "So glad this is almost over!" but for others it is, "What an opportunity this has been—I am going to give it everything I have until the final buzzer!"

Speaking as a veteran spectator, I have often been able to sense which team members are in it until the very end. This includes the ones on the field and the ones on the sidelines. Athletes who are invested in the best interest and welfare of the team are the ones who are still pushing through adversity, still cheering, still high-fiving, still looking for opportunities to score, and still playing tough defense. Toward the end of the game when you watch this caliber of player, you should not be able to tell what the scoreboard says. Whether their team is on their way to chalking up a victory or taking a loss, these athletes are all about team unity, team development, and team improvement.

We have all seen the type of player who quits on his or her teammates. Being a quitter, whether physically, emotionally, or mentally or all of the above, is a self-centered quality. It is a characteristic that says, "I am done. What matters is how I feel." Unfortunately, most of the time this mindset is contagious. Other teammates join in on the sluggish, spiritless style and soon the team is not only battling their opponents, they have a whole new conflict on their hands.

Just as an "I give up" attitude can spread throughout a team, so can the attitude that says, "No matter the outcome, we are going to be relentless in our effort." Have you been in both situations?

I challenge you to be the type of athlete who spurs their teammates on to the finish line. That athlete is the one who is often called upon to be a leader and a motivator. That is the athlete who reflects Christ on the court.

Let us not become weary in doing good, for at the proper time we will reap a harvest if we do not give up. (Galatians 6:9)

Blessed is the one who perseveres under trial because, having stood the test, that person will receive the crown of life that the Lord has promised to those who love him. (James 1:12)

And as for you, brothers and sisters, never tire of doing what is good. (2 Thessalonians 3:13)

Dear Lord, I desire to be an athlete who can be depended on to give my best effort until the very last moment of the contest. Whether I am sitting on the bench or playing on the court, Lord, I pray that I will represent You in the way I conduct myself. May others see determination, perseverance, and hope in me. In Your holy name I pray, Amen.

WINNING
WITH GRACE

When our children played tee ball as six- and seven-year-olds, they were usually told the game had ended in a tie. However, my kids and their friends frequently kept score in the dugout. Despite being told otherwise, they were well aware there was a winning team and a losing team and often informed their parents the exact number of runs scored!

Not keeping score in children's sports has become a more popular practice in recent years. I believe this is a disservice to kids, because they are missing out on real-life lessons! Lessons about losing with dignity, striving to win, and winning with grace are some of the most important aspects of participating in team sports, and they can have a positive lifelong impact.

Unfortunately, there are teams that exude a measure of arrogance when their team is racking up victories in the win column. They show evidence of thinking it is all about them individually instead of about the team as a whole and God Who gave them the opportunities to improve as a team in the first place!

On the other hand, when a team that has learned the life lesson of winning with grace is on a winning streak, you will often see their grateful spirit being demonstrated. They are quick to give credit where credit is due by showing honor to their coaches, teammates, and supporters with their thanks.

Victory is an admirable goal, but it should be put in its rightful place. Team improvement should supersede winning as a team aspiration. However, winning is often a byproduct of the combination of continuous sacrifice and teamwork necessary for improvement to take place.

Proverbs 27:2a says, "Let someone else praise you, not your own mouth...." This is a policy that successful teams are wise to adopt. Focusing on the qualities and abilities that are causing the winning record instead of boasting about the wins themselves is a way to show that you are indeed playing for glory of God and displaying His grace in the process!

Let your conversation be always full of grace, seasoned with salt, so that you may know how to answer everyone. (Colossians 4:6)

But he gives us more grace. That is why Scripture says: "God opposes the proud but shows favor to the humble." (James 4:6)

If it is possible, as far as it depends on you, live at peace with everyone. (Romans 12:18)

Dear Lord, there are times when I can get caught up in the prestige that success and victories can bring. My prayer is that when I am presented with a choice to gloat over a win or to be thankful for the opportunity for my team to be granted success, I will choose a grateful heart that shows others Your amazing grace. In Your holy name I pray, Amen.

I DON'T GET IT

You find yourself looking at the scoreboard as the final seconds tick off the clock. You visualized the outcome of this game at least a hundred times, but not like this. You see the slumping shoulders and downward-pointed eyes among your teammates. You dread the expected handshaking ceremony after the game, because you feel the unwelcome burning of tears threatening to fall.

I have seen our children experience season-ending interceptions in the last seconds of a football playoff game. I have seen a key player's injury basically snuff out the post-season dreams of an undefeated basketball team that our sons were on. I have witnessed our kids trying to make sense of a loss that seemingly came out of nowhere.

Moms desperately want to take heartbreak from their children. I have experienced times of failing to find the words that would do that after dream-ending losses.

I remember our oldest son being an example of grace and looking to Jesus for strength when he endured two heart-wrenching basketball and football season endings his senior year. I remember overhearing our second son console others and tell his little brother, "You really stepped up this year. I'm proud of you," after a season-ending loss his senior year in which their double-digit point third-quarter lead shockingly turned into a loss. I remember our third son posting a thanksgiving-filled social media post of the positive experience of high school sports shortly after his senior basketball season ended sooner than he had hoped. I remember our daughter displaying amazing poise and maturity during a very disappointing time of one of her high school basketball seasons.

Why do your reactions matter when faced with disappointments? Here are three reasons: 1) you are representing your college. You signed a dotted line promising to conduct yourself positively on behalf of that institution; 2) you are representing your family. Most parents do their best to raise their children to be respectful and resilient. When hardship happens, you make your family proud when you handle it with class; 3) you are representing Jesus. He deserves our best reflection. We would probably agree it is easier to display the character of Jesus Christ when things are going well, but when adversity strikes, it can especially impact others if we react to difficult situations by pointing people toward the Kingdom of God.

In every trial, there is an opportunity to show how God will work through it to exhibit His glory. Take advantage of every chance to glorify God!

We *are* hard pressed on every side, but not crushed; perplexed, but not in despair; persecuted, but not abandoned; struck down, but not destroyed. (2 Corinthians 4:8-9)

Consider it pure joy, my brothers and sisters, whenever you face trials of many kinds, because you know that the testing of your faith produces perseverance. Let perseverance finish *its* work so that you may be mature and complete, not lacking anything. (James 1:2-4)

Dear Lord, I realize disappointments can sometimes be part of the college athletic experience. I pray you will help me deal with sadness in a powerful way. I pray that I console others going through difficult situations with words and actions that reveal Your love, comfort, and faithfulness. Help me keep my focus on what is most important: You. In Your holy name I pray, Amen.

OFF-SEASON
WORK

As the wife of a coach, I have heard numerous times about how off-season work can be the difference-maker in a player's success. Once the season begins, the coaching staff is focused on team development, team unity, and team improvement. Obviously, a large component of that is thanks to hard work accomplished by individuals. However, the bulk of what coaches try to achieve during the season is team-oriented. Therefore, individual skill development in the off-season is ultimately up to the individual!

Off-Season work is a choice to put your athletic goals high on your list of priorities. I admire the athletes who realize the advantages of off-season work and consequently make necessary changes to their schedules.

The off-season is the time you can especially make noticeable strides in your skills. When you bring those talents to the in-season practices and competitions, you often see that hard work pays off. Your extra time commitment and extra effort can pay big dividends when the team begins their season.

Matthew 5:41 says, "If anyone forces you to go one mile, go with them two miles." Hence, we have the often-heard phrase, "Go the extra mile." Also, in Colossians 3:23a, the Bible tells us, "Whatever you do, work at it with all your heart." Off-season work is a perfect example of both going the extra mile and working at something with all your heart.

One sign of maturity is setting individual goals and reaching them with the purpose of making the entire team better. Another sign is putting in additional time and effort, all the while realizing that other people are not necessarily going to know about or be overly concerned about your work ethic and extra training! When you set goals for the greater good and you do it without caring whether or not you get credit for it, you have reached an impressive milestone in your athletic career.

If anyone forces you to go one mile, go with them two miles. (Matthew 5:41)

Commit to the LORD whatever you do, and he will establish your plans. (Proverbs 16:3)

Dear Lord, I pray that You will fill me with the desire to go the extra mile. Please grant me the self-discipline, the time, and the energy to put in extra hours in the off-season. I pray You will help me make goals that will benefit my entire team, and that my ambition will be a motivator for others as well. Thank You, Lord, for giving me a chance to get a step ahead by putting in extra effort and time. In Your holy name I pray, Amen.